THE ANIMAL CELL AND DIVISION BIOLOGY FOR KIDS

CHILDREN'S BIOLOGY BOOKS

BABY PROFESSOR

EDUCATION KIDS

Speedy Publishing LLC

40 E. Main St. #1156

Newark, DE 19711

www.speedypublishing.com

Copyright 2016

Let's talk about the structure of life and its divisions. Each living thing on Earth is composed of trillions of cells. Cells are the basic structures of life. Animals and plants are formed when cells are joined together.

Animals are also composed of trillions of cells, like all other living things. In this book, you will learn amazing facts about the animal cell and the cell division.

ANIMAL CELL

PLANT CELL

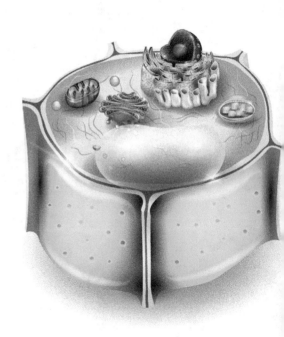

WHAT IS THE DIFFERENCE BETWEEN THE ANIMAL CELL AND THE PLANT CELL?

The plant cell makes the plants independent because it can make its own food while an animal cell is incapable of making its own food.

Nonetheless, an animal cell is considered self-sufficient because it can produce everything it needs. This means that an animal cell is capable of making its own components or structures.

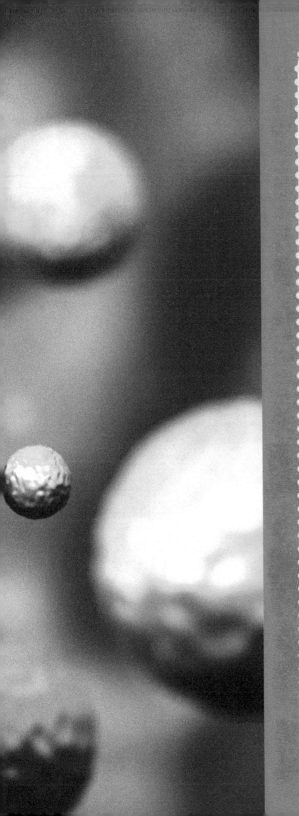

This is because animal cells are composed of nano-chemical factories. An example of this is the Golgi complex which can generate what it needs. It produces its own components.

Each cell in the animal body has its amazing function depending on its type. Animal cells are composed of the main parts, namely: the nucleus, the cell membrane, and the cytoplasm.

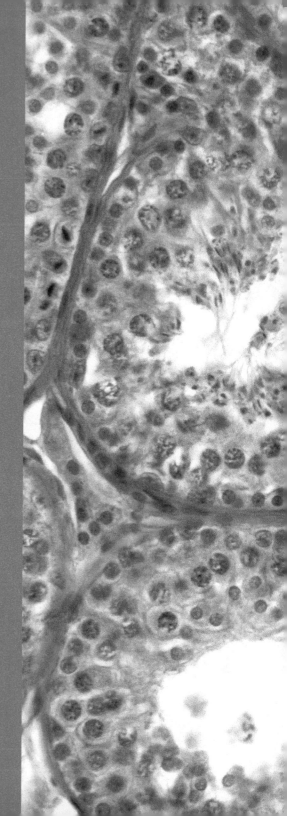

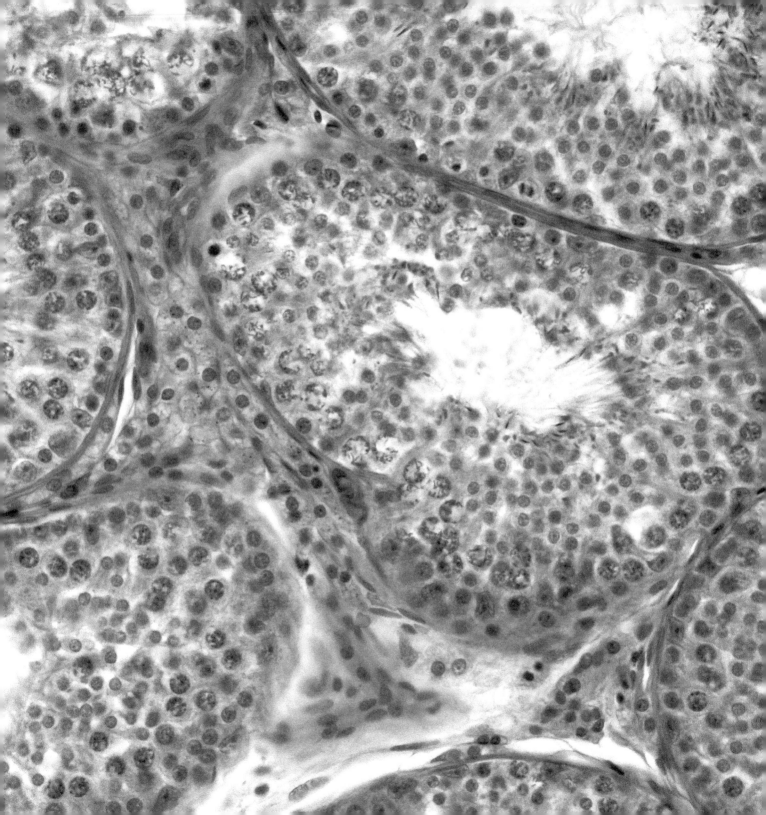

Nucleus

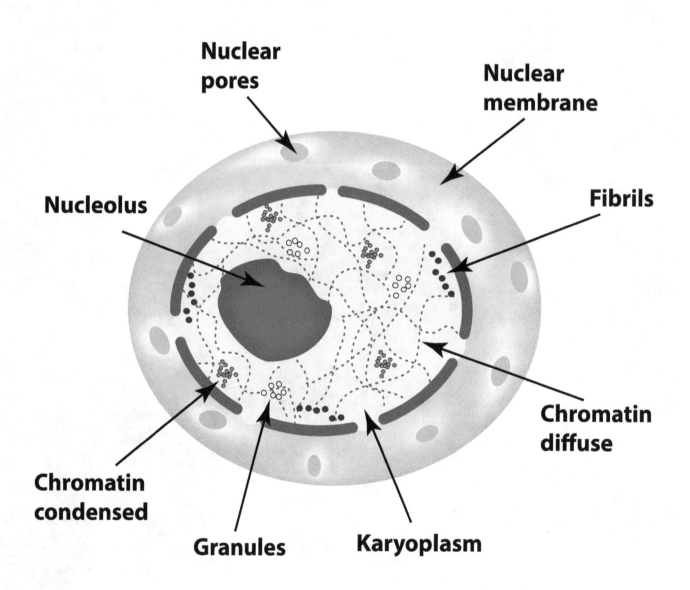

Nuclear pores

Nuclear membrane

Nucleolus

Fibrils

Chromatin diffuse

Chromatin condensed

Granules

Karyoplasm

NUCLEUS

The Nucleus is the brain of the cell. The nucleus is responsible for guiding and giving directions to the cell as to what it will do.

Without the nucleus, the cell could not function. In fact, the nucleus has the capability of making the needed cell organelles. The nucleus is located anywhere in the cell.

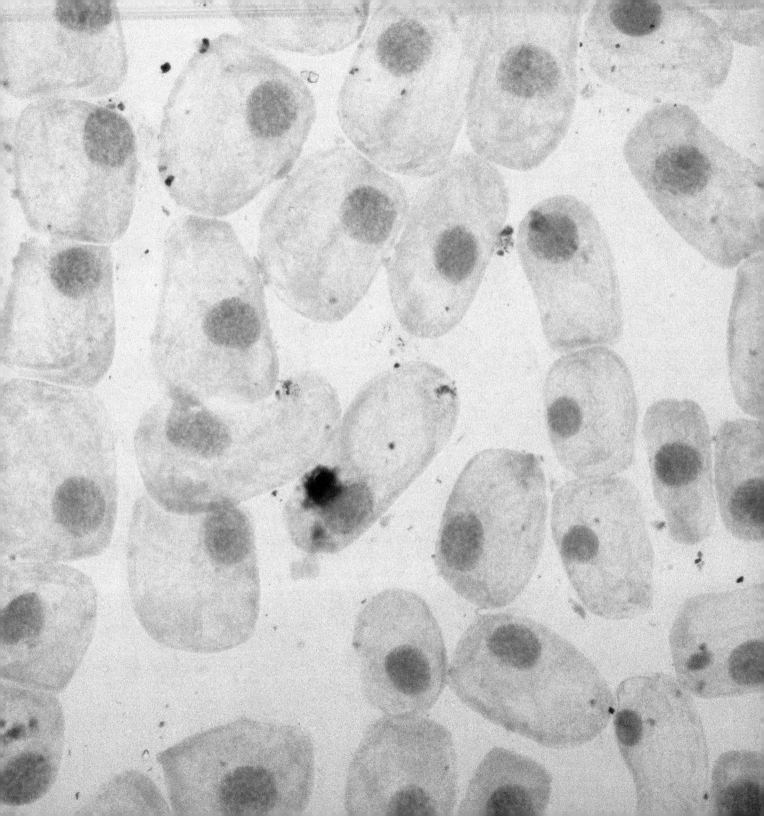

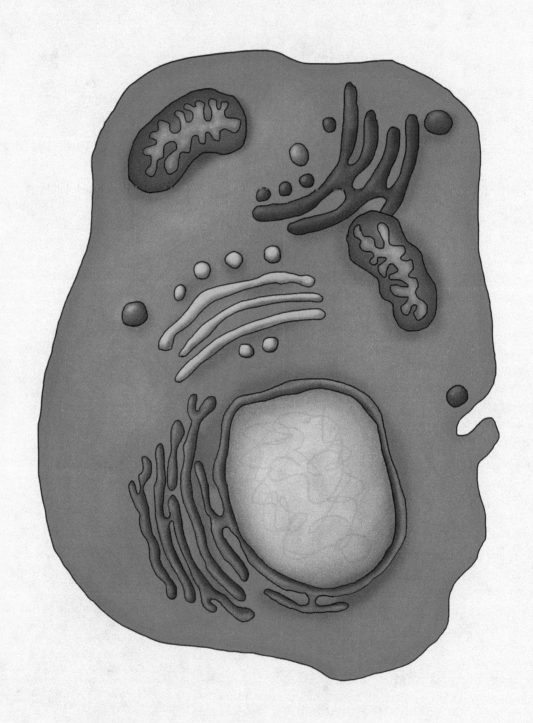

However, it is important to know that only the eukaryotic cells have a nucleus. The nucleus is an organelle that stores the cell's genetic information in the form of DNA or deoxyribonucleic acid.

CELL MEMBRANE

The cell membrane protects the animal cells. It serves as the best guard of the cell. It protects the cell from harmful objects.

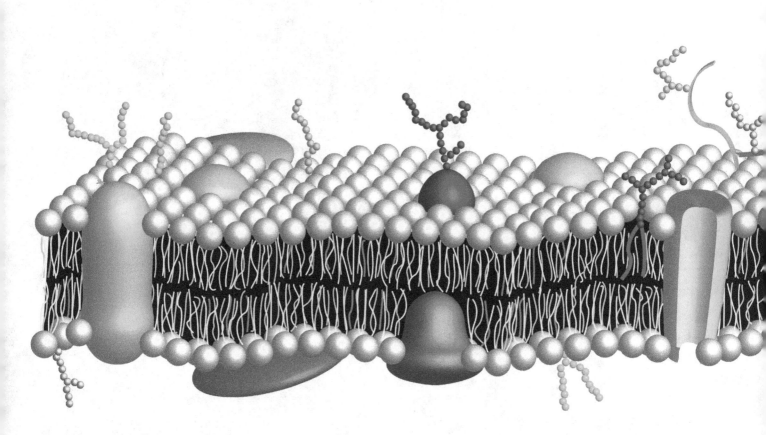

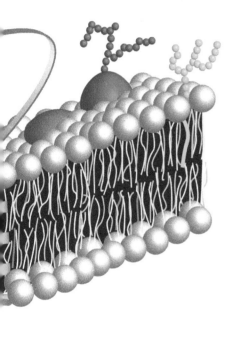

CYTOPLASM

The cytoplasm is responsible for giving shape to the cell. It is the component of the cell that keeps organelles in their places.

It is made of protein. The cytoplasm makes sure the function of the organelles to transport materials is done properly.

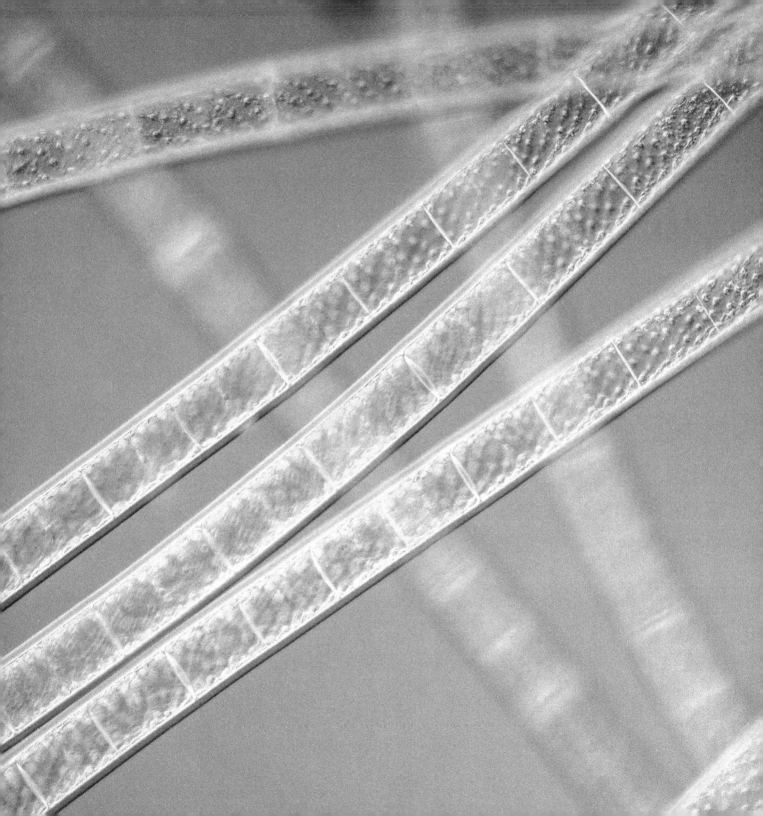

The cytoplasm also helps in breaking down the wastes of the cells. Inside the cytoplasm is a cytoskeleton. Just like the plant cells, animal cells are eukaryotic cells but they are very different in their structures.

A plant cell is bigger than an animal cell. An animal cell comes in diverse sizes and has an irregular shape.

Plant cell

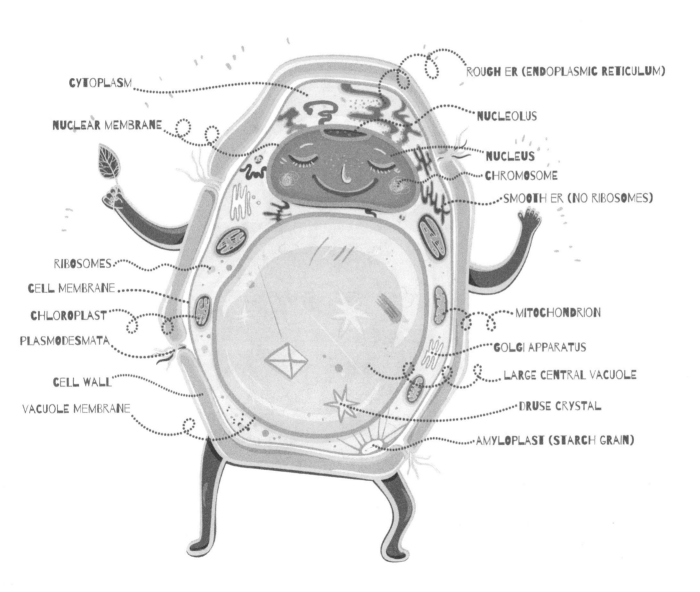

CYTOPLASM

NUCLEAR MEMBRANE

ROUGH ER (ENDOPLASMIC RETICULUM)

NUCLEOLUS

NUCLEUS

CHROMOSOME

SMOOTH ER (NO RIBOSOMES)

RIBOSOMES

CELL MEMBRANE

CHLOROPLAST

PLASMODESMATA

CELL WALL

VACUOLE MEMBRANE

MITOCHONDRION

GOLGI APPARATUS

LARGE CENTRAL VACUOLE

DRUSE CRYSTAL

AMYLOPLAST (STARCH GRAIN)

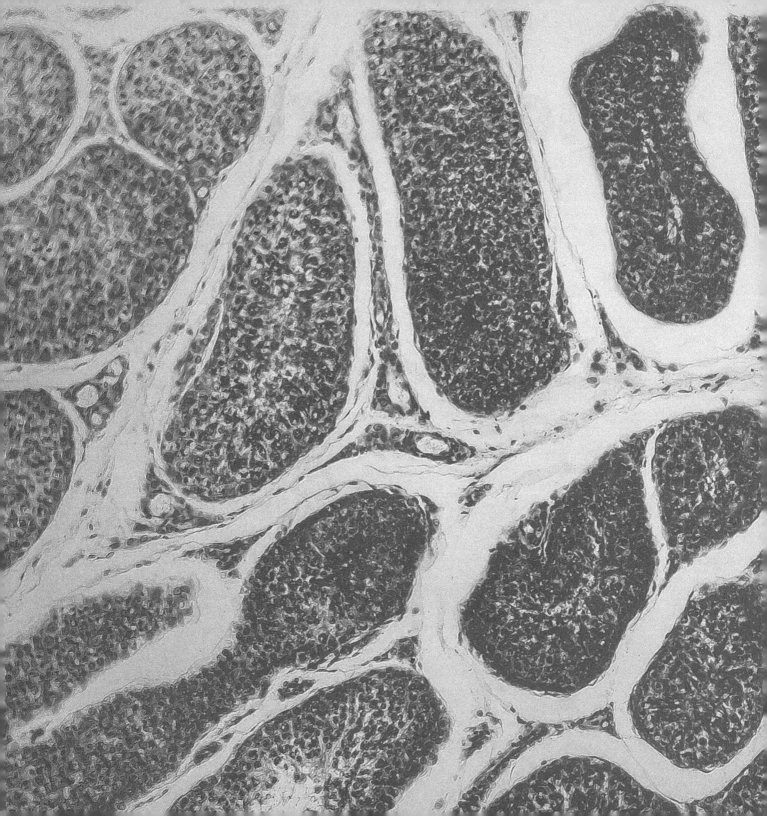

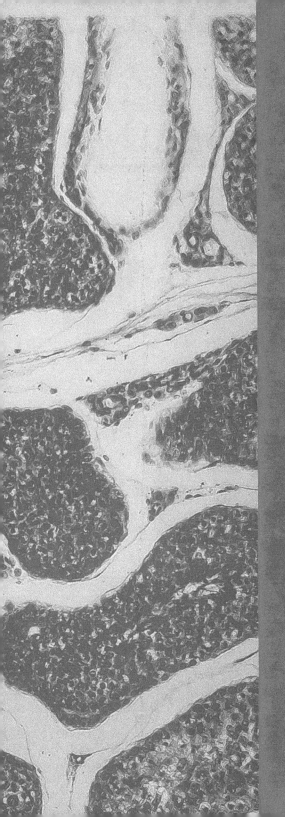

Some animal cells are relatively large while others are very small. However, even the largest of the animal cells can't be seen by the naked eye.

Moreover, an animal cell doesn't have a cell wall. Eukaryotic cells are cells in which the nucleus and organelles are inside the cell membrane. The DNA materials are found in the nucleus.

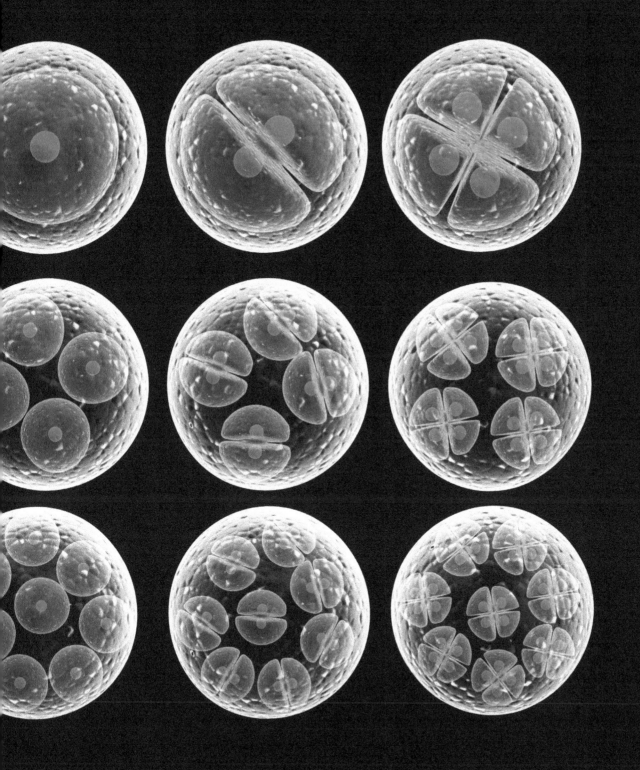

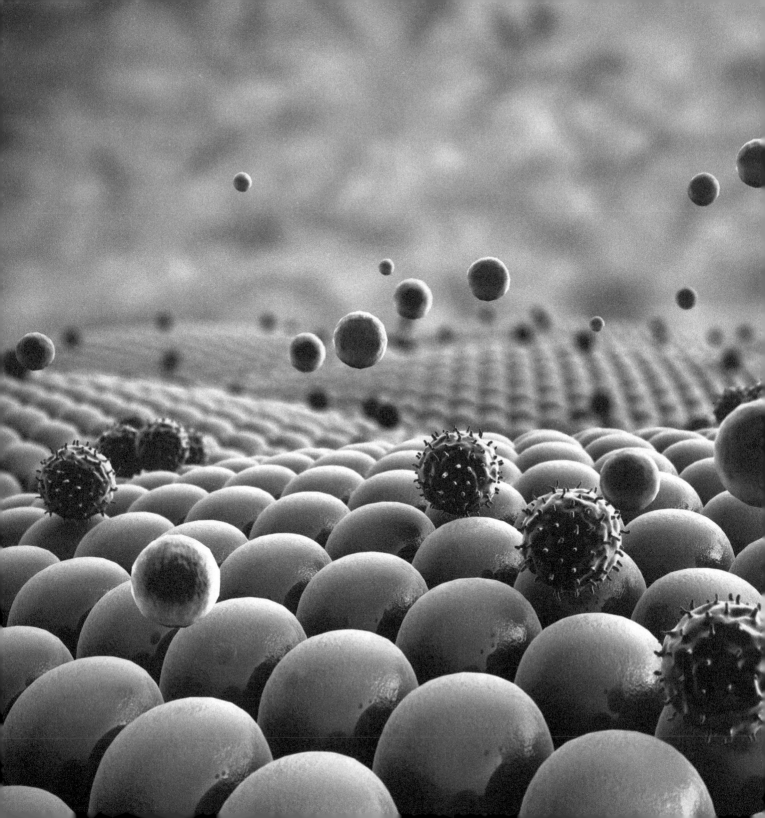

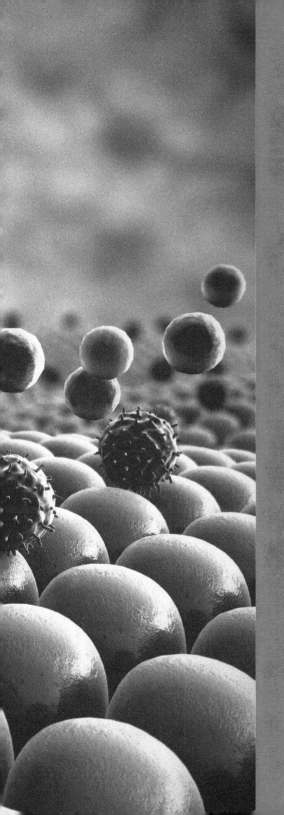

Do you know that animal cells have self-destruction abilities?
This means that they are capable of destroying themselves.

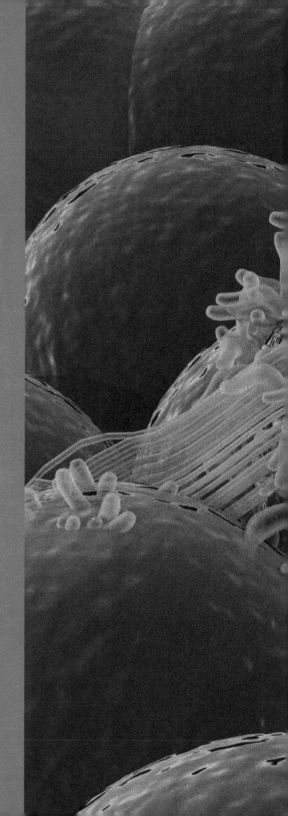

This is done through the process known as Apoptosis or commonly known as "cellular suicide".

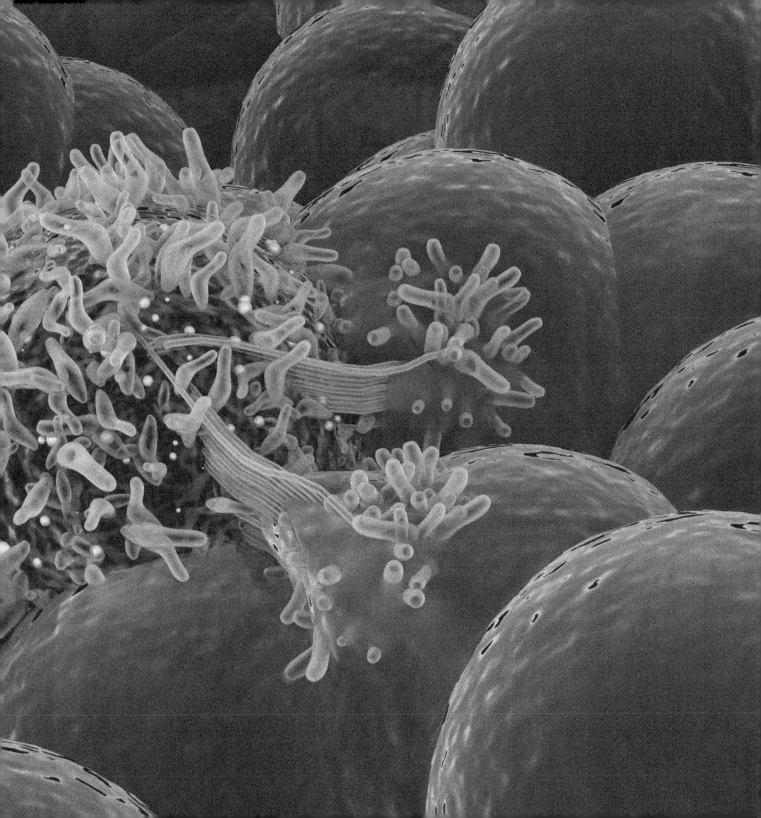

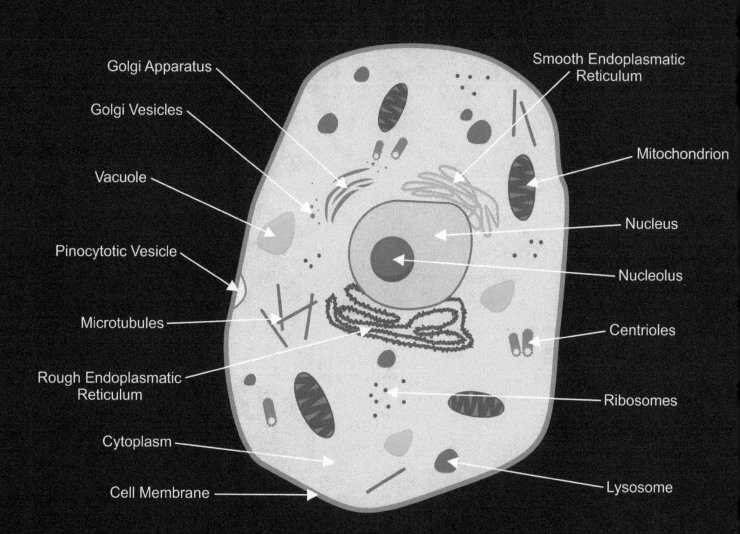

Golgi Apparatus

Golgi Vesicles

Vacuole

Pinocytotic Vesicle

Microtubules

Rough Endoplasmatic Reticulum

Cytoplasm

Cell Membrane

Smooth Endoplasmatic Reticulum

Mitochondrion

Nucleus

Nucleolus

Centrioles

Ribosomes

Lysosome

WHAT ARE ORGANELLES?

Organelles are amazing structures inside the cell which perform different functions. They produce hormones and enzymes. They also provide energy to the cells.

Examples of organelles are centrioles, lysosomes, cilia, and flagella.
An organism is composed of trillions of animal cells.

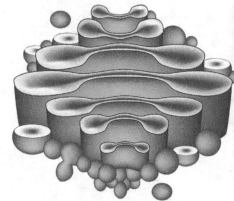

Golgi apparatus

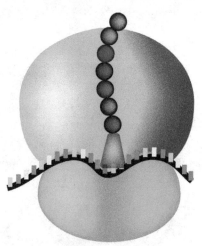

Ribosome

CELL ORGANELLE

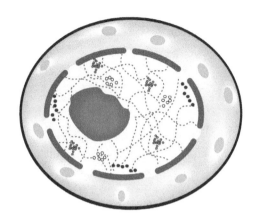

Nucleus

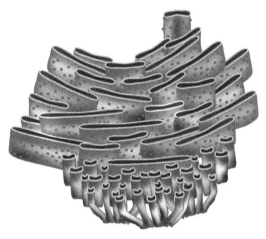

Endoplasmic reticulum

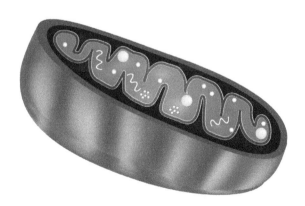

Mitochondrion

Centrosome

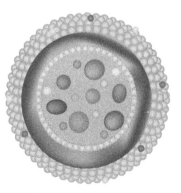

Lysosome

The human body, for example, has many types of animal cells. Each type of cells has amazing biological functions and roles.

REPRODUCTION OF ANIMAL CELLS

Animal cells are reproduced through the process called Mitosis or sexual reproduction. It is the process that involves the ova and the sperm. A new organism is produced when the ova and the sperm meet together in a sexual activity.

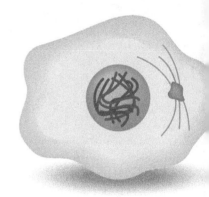

INTERPHASE

ANAP

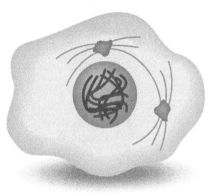

PROPHASE

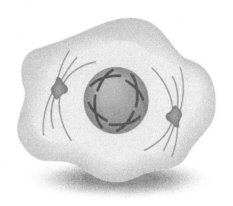

PROMETAPHASE

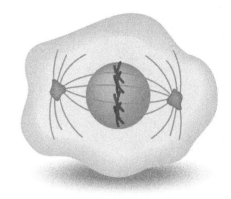

METAPHASE

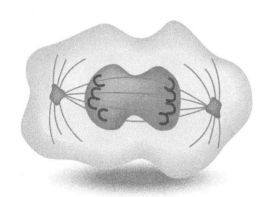

TELOPHASE

**MITOSIS
COMPLETED**

Did you know that an animal cell is an amazing storehouse? It is because an animal cell comprises all the information and genetic material. These things are needed to make the new organism grow.

In other words, a single animal cell contains the information about biological make-up of an organism including all the traits of an organism.

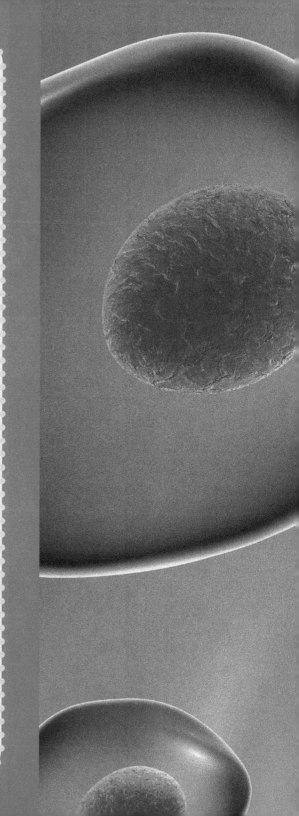

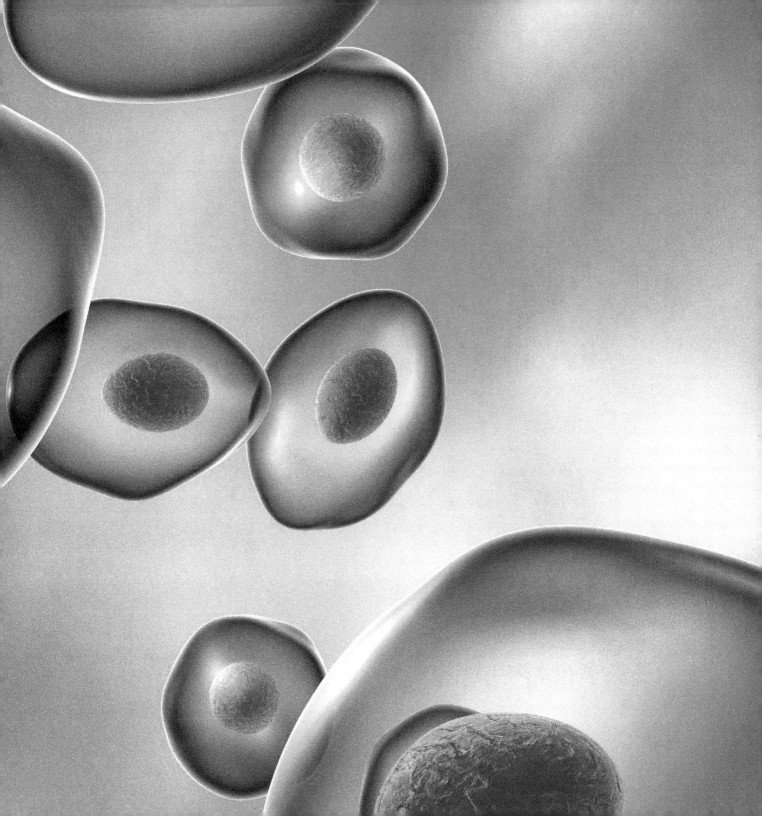

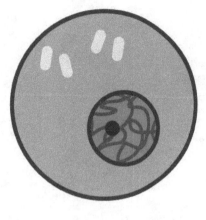

INTERPHASE

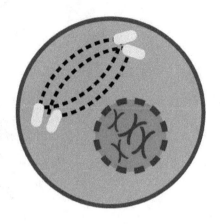

PROPHASE

ANAPHASE

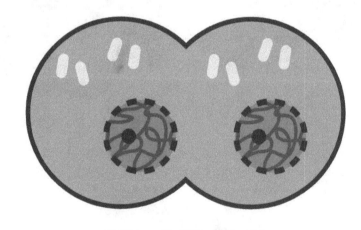

TELOPHASE

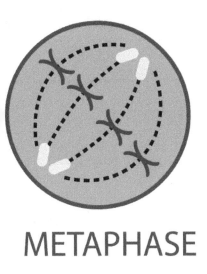

METAPHASE

DAUGHTER
CELLS

NOW, LET'S TALK ABOUT ANIMAL CELL DIVISION.

It is believed that every organism undergoes cell division. Every multi-cellular organism all begin as a fertilized egg.

Eukaryotic cells go through two different types of cell division. In other words, plants, animals, and fungi cells are capable of cell division. These are Meiosis and Mitosis. These are quick yet very complex processes.

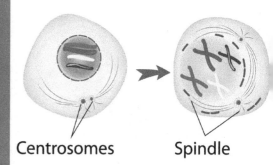

Interphase   **Prophase**

Centrosomes   Spindle

Cell division (meiosis)

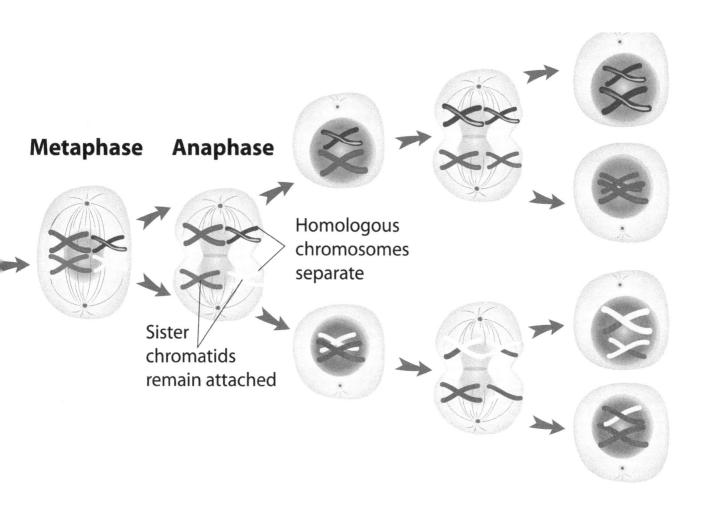

Metaphase **Anaphase**

Homologous
chromosomes
separate

Sister
chromatids
remain attached

Cell division (mitosis)

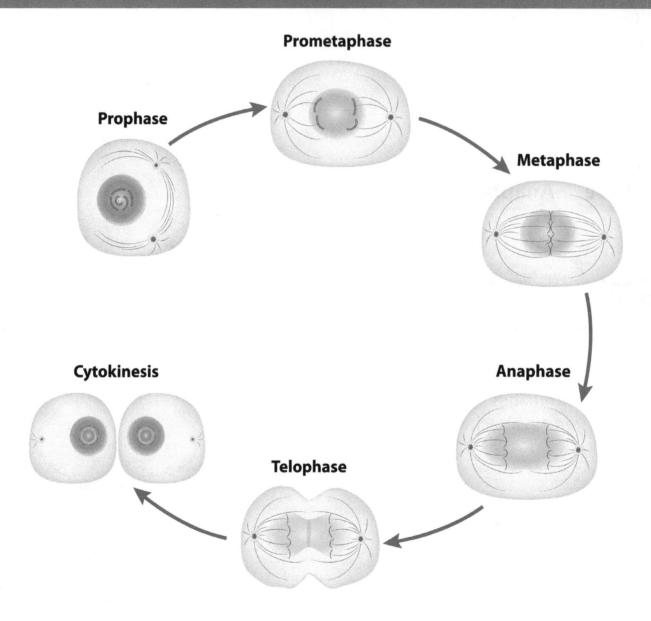

Prophase

Prometaphase

Metaphase

Anaphase

Telophase

Cytokinesis

WHAT IS MITOSIS?

It is a type of cell division in which the chromosomes are duplicated. It means an identical copy of them. The chromosomes are scattered equally to the daughter cells.

This equal distribution is known as Equational division. Mitosis is divided into five stages. These are the prophase, prometaphase, metaphase, anaphase, and telophase.

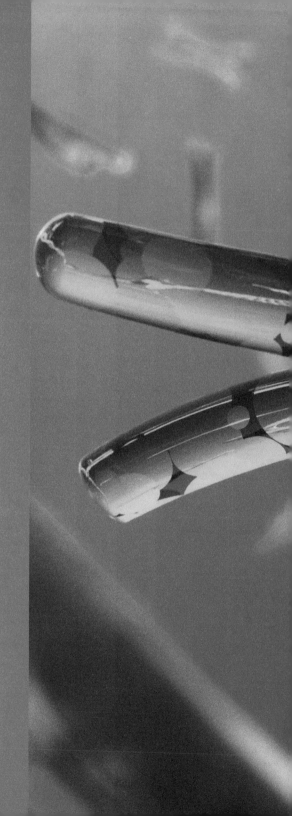

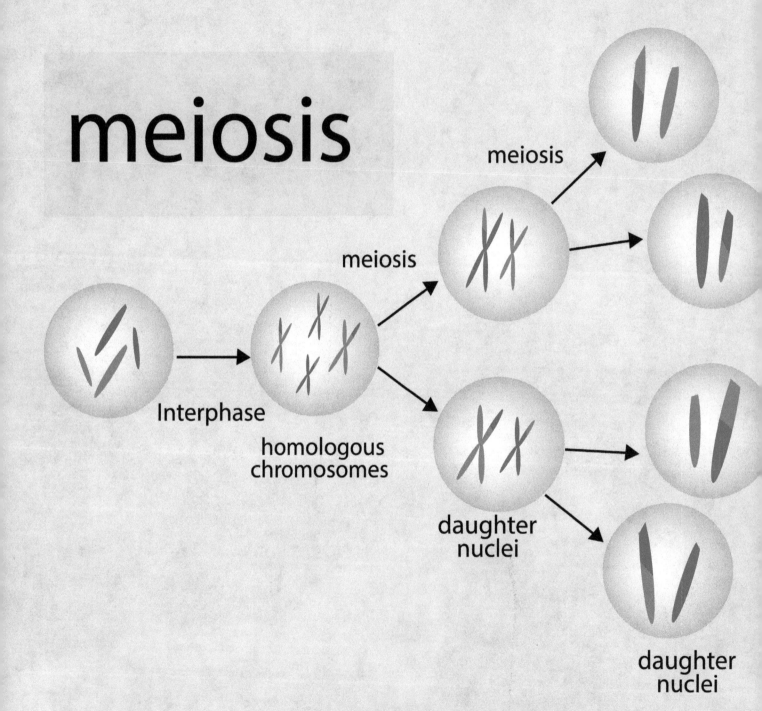

meiosis

Interphase

homologous
chromosomes

meiosis

meiosis

daughter
nuclei

daughter
nuclei

WHAT IS MEIOSIS?

Meiosis is a specialized cell division in which chromosomes are copied and paired up. The paired chromosomes are then separated to create eggs or sperm through sexual reproduction.

It is a process in which the unique genetic information of two parents is combined. It produces reproductive cells. Examples are egg cells, sperm cells, and spores for plants and fungi.

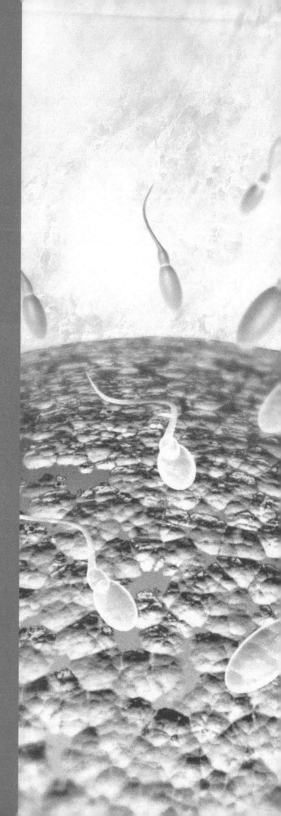

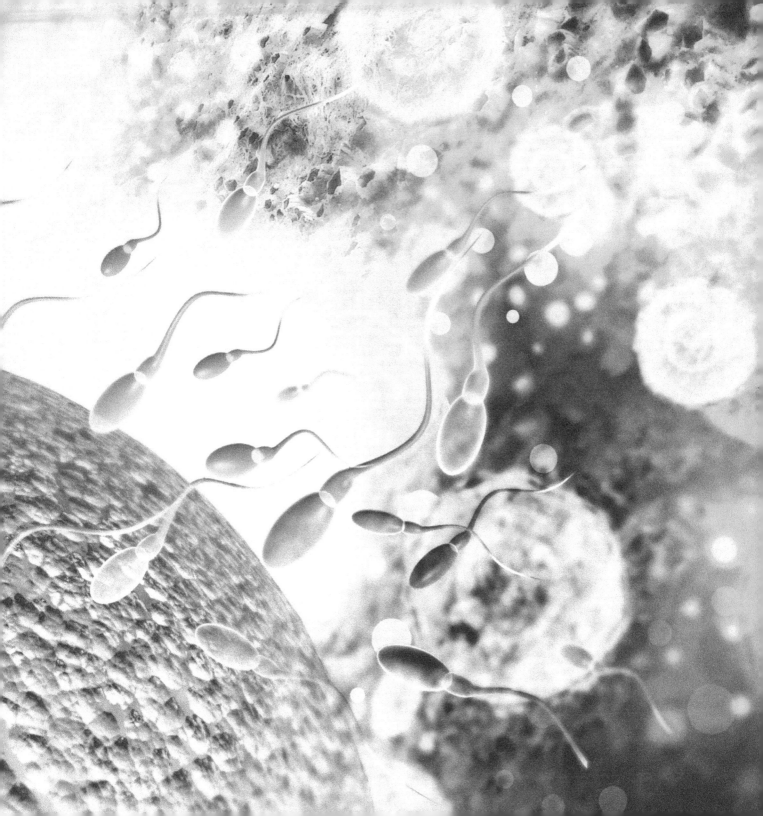

Every living organism on Earth contains amazing structures which originate exactly from a single cell. It just shows how mysterious life is.

CPSIA information can be obtained
at www.ICGtesting.com
Printed in the USA
BVHW011725230320
575726BV00009BA/218